TALES
from
Around the World

Oxford Progressive English Readers provide a wide range of enjoyable reading at six language levels. Text lengths range from 8,000 words at the Starter level, to about 35,000 words at Level 5. The latest methods of text analysis, using specially designed software, ensure that readability is carefully controlled.

The aim of the series is to present stories to engage the interest of the reader; to intrigue, mystify, amuse, delight and stimulate the imagination.

FOLK TALES

from
Around the World

Retold by Rosemary Border

OXFORD
UNIVERSITY PRESS

OXFORD
UNIVERSITY PRESS

Oxford University Press is a department of the University of Oxford.
It furthers the University's objective of excellence in research, scholarship,
and education by publishing worldwide. Oxford is a registered trade mark of
Oxford University Press in the UK and in certain other countries

Published in Hong Kong by
Oxford University Press (China) Limited
18th Floor, Warwick House East, Taikoo Place, 979 King's Road, Quarry Bay,
Hong Kong

© Oxford University Press (China) Limited 2005

The moral rights of the author have been asserted

First Edition published in 2005

ISBN: 978-0-19-597147-7

13 15 17 19 20 18 16 14

Acknowledgements:
Illustrated by Wildman
Retold by Rosemary Border
Syllabus design and text analysis by David Foulds

Contents

Introduction

The stories in this book come from many parts of the world.

Germany

In Hamelin there is an old house called the *Rattenfängerhaus* — the Rat-catcher's House. On one wall of the house is a poem. *The Pied Piper of Hamelin* tells the story of a piper in a red and yellow robe. He led 130 of Hamelin's children away, and nobody ever saw them again. The name Pied Piper comes from a long English poem by Robert Browning.

The USA

Rip Van Winkle was the laziest man in the village. One day he fell asleep — and he slept for twenty years! Until 1776, George III was King of England. He was also King of the American colonies. In 1776, the colonies wanted to rule themselves. There was a lot of fighting and a lot of arguing, but Rip did not know about that because he was asleep!

Britain

Dick Whittington tells the story of a poor boy and his cat. The cat made Dick a rich man. He became Lord Mayor of London. There was a real Dick Whittington. He became Lord Mayor of London too. Did he have a cat? Nobody knows!

Japan
Have you ever got into trouble for drawing on walls or in books? In Japan, a boy could not stop himself from drawing dragons — on walls, on floors, on pieces of paper. One day those dragons saved the boy's life. How did they do that? Read *The Boy Who Drew Dragons* and find the answer.

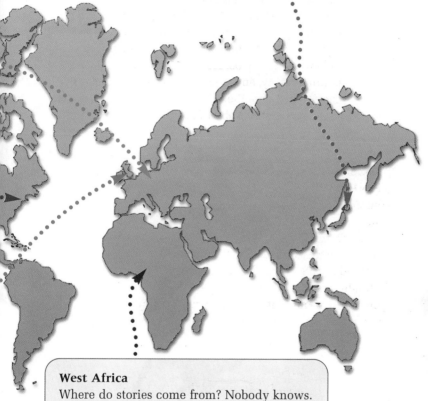

West Africa
Where do stories come from? Nobody knows. The last story in the book comes from Africa. It is called *Where Do Stories Come From?* A mother visits the Land of the Magic People. She brings back the first story.

1
The Pied Piper of Hamelin:
Part One

Rats!

Promises are very important. It is easy to make a promise about something. 'I promise to wash the dishes, Mum.' Or 'I won't tell your secret — I promise!' It is not always easy to keep that promise. But you must do your best to keep it. You must wash those dishes. You must not tell that secret to anyone. If you break your promise, something bad usually happens. This is the story of a broken promise.

This story happened a long time ago. There was a town called Hamelin. It was a beautiful place. There were pretty houses with red roofs and flower gardens. There was a big market place and busy shops. And there was a wide river with a stone bridge.

For many years Hamelin was a good place to live. And then the rats came! Where did the rats come from? Why did they choose Hamelin? Nobody knows. But they came. Soon the town was full of them.

Rats! They came into the houses and shops. They found their way into cupboards. They made holes in bags of food. They made their nests everywhere. The rats were big and strong. They had sharp claws and long yellow teeth. They were not afraid of anything or anybody. Nobody was safe. Dogs and cats ran away when they saw them.

'We want to see the Mayor!'

One day an enormous rat attacked a baby. A crowd of angry people went to the Town Hall. 'We want to see the Mayor!' they shouted.

The Mayor was a fat little man. He liked being the Mayor of Hamelin. It made him feel important. He liked wearing beautiful robes. He really liked his hat with a big white feather. He enjoyed eating enormous dinners with the mayors of other towns. But he was a lazy man, too. He liked being a mayor but he didn't like to do any work. Now he did not know what to do.

'What are you going to do about the rats?'

'You have to do something!' shouted an old man.

'That's right,' said a woman. 'We pay for your robes and your dinners. Now you must do something for us!'

The baby's mother showed her child to the Mayor. There were bites on the baby's hands and face. 'Look at my baby,' she said angrily. 'What are you going to do about this?'

The Mayor was a parent too. He felt very sad about the baby. But he was not a clever man. He really did not know what to do or say.

'Good people,' the Mayor began, 'this is a difficult time. We must all work together ...'

'You're the Mayor!' shouted an old man. 'You must get rid of the rats — quickly. If you don't, we'll choose a new Mayor!'

'Leave it to me,' said the Mayor. 'Now please go home. I'll think of something.'

The silver pipe

The Mayor and his councillors sat around a big table. They talked and talked for hours. How could they get rid of the rats? Nobody knew. There were too many. And they were too big and strong.

Then suddenly there was a knock at the door.

'Who's that?' said the Mayor. He looked frightened. 'Is it a rat?'

'Rats don't usually knock,' said one of the councillors. He got up and opened the door.

A tall, thin stranger came into the room. He had long yellow hair and big blue eyes. He wore a long red and yellow robe. The man smiled. His eyes shone like diamonds.

'I am the Pied Piper,' said the stranger. 'I have heard about the rats. They're giving you a lot of trouble. I can get rid of them for you.'

'How can you do that?' asked one of the councillors.

'With this,' said the stranger quietly.

Now they noticed a string around his neck. On the string was a long silver pipe.

'This is a special pipe,' he said. 'When your rats hear my music, they will follow me. They will follow me to their death.' He looked at the Mayor. 'If I get rid of the rats,' he said, 'will you give me a thousand dollars?'

'Yes, yes!' shouted the Mayor. 'We promise! Please start at once.'

2

The Pied Piper of Hamelin:

Part Two

Magical music

The Pied Piper stepped out into the street. He saw rats everywhere. He smiled. Then he began to play his pipe.

Magical music came out of that silver pipe. The rats lifted their heads and listened. Then, one by one, they came out of their nests. They ran towards the music. Hundreds of rats came running out of the shops and houses. At first the Pied Piper walked slowly. Then he began to run. And then he began to dance. And all the time he played his pipe.

The Mayor looked out of his window. He saw the Pied Piper dancing along. Rats followed him. They were all dancing to the strange, magical music. The Pied Piper led the rats to the river Weser.

They all jumped into the fast-running water. They could not swim. Every one of them died.

The people of Hamelin laughed and sang and shouted. The dogs and cats came out of their hiding places. They were not frightened now. The Mayor stood on the steps of the Town Hall. He talked quickly and gave orders.

'Quick!' he said. 'Get rid of the rats' nests. Make everything clean and tidy again. Then tonight there will be a party. There will be singing and dancing, eating and drinking. I am a hero. I have got rid of the rats!'

A broken promise

'Excuse me, Mr Mayor,' said a voice beside him. 'Have you forgotten something?'

'Forgotten something?' said the Mayor. He looked surprised.

'I promised to get rid of the rats — which I did. And you promised to give me a thousand dollars.'

'Oh!' The Mayor stopped smiling. A thousand dollars was a lot of money. He could buy a lot of new robes. He could enjoy a lot of enormous dinners, too.

'Just a minute,' said the Mayor. He spoke quietly to his councillors.

'Do we really need to give this man a thousand dollars? He's got rid of the rats. He can't bring them back!'

'We agree,' said the councillors.

The Mayor turned to the Pied Piper.

'A thousand dollars? I didn't mean it. But you have done a good job. Here, take fifty dollars.'

The Pied Piper was angry. 'I can't waste time arguing with you. I must go to Baghdad tomorrow to get rid of some snakes. If you break your promise, you'll be very sorry.'

The Mayor laughed. 'I don't think so! You've got rid of the rats. You can't bring them back again. Go to Baghdad. Here, take your money.' He threw a small bag ⁵ of money towards the Pied Piper. The Pied Piper let the bag fall to the ground. He turned and walked away.

The door in the mountain

For the second time, the Pied Piper stepped into the street. Again he began to play his pipe. The music was happy and cheerful. This time, boys and girls came out of the houses. They followed the magical music.

Their parents could not stop them. They could not move or speak. Their children jumped and danced. They followed the Pied Piper. He led them towards the high mountain just outside the town.

'They must stop soon,' said one of the mothers. 'They can't climb that mountain.'

She was right. The mountain was too high for the children to climb. But suddenly a strange thing happened. The side of the mountain opened like a door. The Pied Piper danced through the doorway. All the children followed him. Then the door shut with a bang behind them. All the children were inside the mountain. All except one little boy with a bad leg. He was too slow. At last he came to the door — but it was shut. He sat on the ground and cried.

Hamelin was never the same again. The Mayor sent people to look for the Pied Piper. He told them to say: 'We're sorry. You can have your thousand dollars. Please bring our children back!'

But the people <u>returned</u>, tired and sad. Nobody saw the Pied Piper, or the children, again.

3

Rip Van Winkle:

Part One

A Dutch colony

In 1609, Hendrick Hudson went on a journey. He sailed from the Netherlands to America. His ship was called the *Half Moon*. He sailed up a beautiful, wide river. He named it the Hudson River.

Some years later, thirty families left the Netherlands. They sailed across the sea. They went to live in America. They started a colony beside the Hudson River. They called their colony the New Netherlands.

They worked hard. They grew crops in the fields. They built houses and churches. More families joined them. Soon there were villages and towns. The biggest town was called New Amsterdam. Peter Stuyvesant was the first mayor.

Then in 1664, ships full of English soldiers came. They attacked the town. The mayor wanted to fight, but the people did not. So the New Netherlands became an English colony.

There were a few changes. New Amsterdam became New York. There was new money. It had a picture of the English King's head on it. The government, under the English King, ruled the land. They told the people the rules for living in the colony. But England was a long way away. So life was much the same. Then some English families arrived. Everyone lived quietly together. More than a hundred years passed.

The laziest man in the village

Beside the Hudson River, you can see the Catskill Mountains. They are very beautiful. There is something magical about them, too. The mountains change colour
5 with the seasons and the weather. Old men look at the mountains to tell what the weather will be like. They say, 'The mountains are blue and purple today. We'll have sunny weather tomorrow.'

At the bottom of those mountains was a village. In
10 this village there lived a farmer called Rip Van Winkle. He lived in a little house with his wife. They had a son called Rip and a daughter called Judith.

Rip Van Winkle was a cheerful, friendly man. He was always happy to help his friends and neighbours.
15 He did little jobs for the women. He helped the men on their farms. The children in the village loved him. He was never too busy to play with them. He told them stories, and he made toys for them.

Everybody in the village loved Rip — except his
20 own wife. She thought he was the laziest man in the village.

Well, in some ways Rip was very hard-working. He spent a lot of time helping other people. But Rip did not like working on his own farm. The buildings fell down.

The children never had new clothes. Mrs Van Winkle argued and shouted at her husband. But Rip just smiled and said nothing.

The King's Head

Rip's best friend was his dog. The dog's name was Wolf. Mrs Van Winkle did not like Wolf.

'That dog is as lazy as you are, Rip!' shouted Mrs Van Winkle. She picked up a brush and waved it angrily. Wolf ran away.

'You never do any work. Nothing grows on our farm. Where are you going? No, you can't leave now! I haven't finished talking to you!'

But Rip and Wolf had already left the house. They were on their way to the village inn.

The inn was called The King's Head. Outside the inn was a tall post with a wooden sign. On the sign was a picture of King George. The innkeeper's name was above the door. It said: The King's Head: Nicholas Vedder. The innkeeper was almost as lazy as Rip.

The inn was a cheerful place. Outside was an old tree with seats under it. On sunny days the men of the village sat and talked for hours. Sometimes travellers came through the village. Sometimes they left an old newspaper behind. Derrick Van Bummel was the schoolteacher. He always read the newspaper to his friends. Rip and Wolf often joined them.

Mrs Van Winkle went
to find Rip. She went to the inn. She knew he would be
there.

'Here you are, Rip!' she said. 'You lazy man! And
5 Nicholas Vedder, you're as lazy as he is! Come home,
Rip. Do some work!'

But Rip did not want to go home. He did not want to
do any work. Sometimes he would say, 'I'm coming,
dear.' But he didn't go home. He went out hunting with
10 Wolf.

4

Rip Van Winkle:

Part Two

A stranger

One afternoon, Rip and Wolf were hunting in the mountains. There were rabbits in Rip's bag. Rip was tired. He sat down on a little green hill under some trees. On one side he could see the Hudson River, far below. On the other side was a deep, dark valley full of rocks. Rip looked up at the sun.

'It will be dark soon, Wolf,' he said sadly. 'We must go home.'

Just then Rip heard a voice. 'Rip Van Winkle! Rip Van Winkle!' He looked round. He could not see anyone.

'I must be dreaming,' he thought. He began to walk towards his home. Then he heard the voice again. 'Rip Van Winkle!'

Wolf gave a low growl. He looked down into the valley. Rip looked too. He saw a

man moving about in the middle of the rocks. Rip was surprised to see anyone there.

'Perhaps it's one of my neighbours. Perhaps he needs help,' thought Rip. 'Come on, Wolf,' he said. 'Let's go down and see.'

Wolf growled again. He and Rip did not know the man. The stranger was short and square-looking. He had thick grey hair and a grey beard. His clothes were strange and old-fashioned. He wore blue trousers with buttons down the sides. His blue-grey coat had a thick belt around the middle. He was carrying a small
15 wooden barrel. He waved to Rip.

A game of ninepins

'He needs help,' thought Rip. He walked up to the man and helped him carry the barrel. Together they climbed up the hill, along the dry bed of a stream.

20 There was a noise like thunder a long way away. The noise came from another valley between dark rocks. 'Thunder,' thought Rip. But the sky was blue and there was no rain.

They climbed and climbed. At last they came to a
25 small valley. There were high walls of rock all round it. Rip saw nine or ten men. All the men had beards. And they all wore strange, old-fashioned clothes, like the stranger. They were playing ninepins with big wooden balls. The men took it in turns to roll a heavy ball
30 towards a group of pins. The heavy ball made a noise like thunder.

One of them looked more important than the others. He was a tall old man. He wore a tall hat with a big feather. He wore a blue coat, and he had a sword in his belt. His socks were red. And his shoes had big round red buttons like flowers.

5

'They look like the people in the old picture on the inn wall,' thought Rip. The picture showed a crowd of Dutchmen in old-fashioned clothes.

The barrel of liquor

10

Rip watched the men playing. Nobody talked or laughed. The only sound was the noise of the balls rolling along and hitting the ninepins. Rip began to feel afraid. 'Why didn't they speak?'

The old man Rip had helped put the barrel down on the ground. The other men left their game and came to join him. They brought old-fashioned cups.

15

The man in the tall hat made a sign to Rip. Rip understood. He turned the tap on the barrel and filled the cups. There was liquor in the barrel. The men drank without speaking.

5　　Rip tasted the liquor. It was strong and sweet. 'This is good,' he said to himself. He poured some more, and drank it. The men finished their drinks. Then they went back to their game. Rip watched them playing for a while.

10　　'I'm feeling a little tired. I think I'll go to sleep.' He lay down on the ground. He shut his eyes, and fell into a deep sleep.

5

Rip Van Winkle:

Part Three

Rip wakes up

Rip woke up. He was on the little green hill under the trees. It was a sunny morning. He could hear birds singing. 'Where am I?' he said to himself. 'Where are those men in their old-fashioned clothes? And the barrel? And the ninepins?'

Rip remembered the small valley with its high walls of rock. He remembered the strange men. He remembered their old-fashioned clothes. He remembered the ninepins. And he remembered the barrel of liquor. 'That drink was very strong,' he thought. 'I've slept all night. What am I going to tell my wife?'

Rip called for Wolf, but the dog did not come. There was an old gun on the ground beside him. It was very dirty and rusty. 'This isn't my gun,' said Rip. 'Perhaps those men took my gun and left this nasty old one. Perhaps they took Wolf too. Well, I'll find them. They must give me my dog and my gun back.'

Rip got a surprise. He remembered the dry stream bed. But now the stream was full of water. He found the high walls of rock, but he could not find a way into the small valley.

Rip was sad to lose his dog and his gun. But he wanted his breakfast. 'Well, I'll go home,' he said to himself. 'But my wife is going to be really angry.'

Rip goes home

On his way to the village, many people looked at Rip. They looked surprised. Dogs growled at him. A crowd of children saw him. Rip did not know any of them.

5 One boy laughed and pointed at Rip.

'Look at the funny man!' he shouted. 'Look at his old-fashioned clothes!'

'Look at his funny old gun!' said a little girl. 'And look at his beard!'

10 Rip put his hand up to his face. His beard was a foot long.

He looked around him. He looked at the Catskill Mountains and the Hudson River. They looked the same. Then he came into the village. But the village

15 looked different. There were a lot of new houses.

'What's happening?' thought Rip. 'Why has everything changed?'

He found the way to his own house. But there was no glass in the windows. A tree grew out of a hole in the

20 roof. A dog lay outside the house. It looked like Wolf. 'Here, Wolf,' called Rip. The dog growled and ran away. 'This is a sad day for me,' thought Rip. 'My own dog doesn't know me!'

Rip went into his house and called for his wife and children. But no voice answered. The house was empty.

Everything is different

'I'll go to The King's Head,' he said to himself.

As Rip walked to the inn, he saw more new houses. 'Well, they weren't there yesterday,' thought Rip. 'I don't understand why everything has changed.'

The old inn looked different too. Above the door were these words: The Washington Hotel: Jonathan Doolittle. 'How strange,' thought Rip. 'The innkeeper's name has changed. What about my friend, Nicholas Vedder?'

Rip looked for the old tree with the seats under it. It was not there. A tall post stood in front of the inn. At the top of the post was a red, white and blue flag. 'I've never seen a flag like that before,' thought Rip.

5

The inn sign was different too. The sign showed a man on a horse. He had a sword in his hand. And on the sign was the name GEORGE WASHINGTON.

There was a small crowd near the door, but Rip did not know any of them. Where were his friends? Where were his kind, friendly neighbours? These people looked very busy and excited. A tall, thin man was speaking to the crowd. He talked about the new government, under President George Washington. Rip heard his words, but he did not understand a thing. 'What does he mean?' thought Rip. 'King George the Third rules this colony.'

6
Rip Van Winkle:
Part Four

'What's happening?'

Suddenly the tall man pointed at Rip. The small crowd looked at Rip.

'What a funny beard,' cried a woman.

'Who are you?' shouted the tall man. 'What are you doing here? Why are you carrying a gun?'

The small crowd looked at Rip. Small children looked frightened and hid behind their parents.

'I — I don't understand,' said Rip. 'I live here. Who are you? And where are all my old neighbours? Where's Nicholas Vedder?'

An old man said sadly, 'Nicholas Vedder died eighteen years ago.'

'Where's Derrick Van Bummel, the schoolteacher?'

'Oh, he went away a long time ago.'

'I don't understand. Why has everything changed? Does anyone know Rip Van Winkle?' asked Rip.

'Oh yes! Look, there he is,' said someone, pointing to a young man.

Rip looked at the young man. It was like looking in a mirror.

'There must be a mistake,' said Rip. 'I'm Rip Van Winkle. What's happening? I went hunting yesterday. I met a group of men playing ninepins in the mountains. I drank too much liquor and I fell asleep. I woke up this morning and everything was different. I can't find my wife, and I can't find my dog ... I don't understand!'

The people looked at each other and shook their heads sadly. 'What a strange man,' they thought.

Just then a young woman pushed through the crowd. She had a baby in her arms. The baby saw Rip's
5 long beard and began to cry.

'Don't cry,' said the young woman. 'The old man isn't going to hurt you.'

The end of the story

'What is your name?' Rip Van Winkle asked the young
10 woman.

'Judith Gardener.'

'And what is your father's name?'

'Rip Van Winkle. Twenty years ago he went out with his dog and his gun. But his dog came home without
15 him. I was a little girl then.'

'And where is your mother?' asked Rip.

'She died last year.'

'Dear Judith, I am your father!' said Rip. He looked around him. 'Does anybody know me? Does anybody
20 remember Rip Van Winkle?'

An old lady came forward. 'Yes, I do. I know you. Welcome home, old friend.'

Then old Peter Vanderdonk pushed through the crowd. 'Welcome home, Rip. You left home twenty years ago. Where have you been?'

Rip told everyone what had happened that night. Everyone thought Rip's story was very strange.

'Poor Rip — he's foolish — or he's lying,' the people said. But old Peter knew a lot about the early days of the colony.

'Rip isn't telling lies,' he said. 'Strange things happen in the Catskill Mountains. The mountains are magical. They say Hendrick Hudson and his sailors come back to the mountains. They return just for one day, in every twenty years. My father told me he saw them once in their old-fashioned Dutch clothes. And I once heard the sound of their balls and ninepins. The sound is just like thunder.'

Rip's daughter Judith and her husband asked Rip to live with them. He enjoyed playing with his little grandson. He also enjoyed sitting outside the inn with his friends. He enjoyed telling his strange story. Travellers going through the village would ask him all about his adventure.

Sometimes, on a summer evening, there was the sound of thunder in the mountains. Then the old people of the village said, 'Hendrick Hudson and his men have come back. They are playing ninepins again!'

7
The Boy Who Drew Dragons:
Part One

The boy goes to the temple

In Japan, many years ago, there lived a boy. This boy
lived with his parents and his older brother and
sister. They lived on a farm and grew crops.

5   One autumn all the crops died in the fields. Nobody
could understand it. The weather was not too hot or too
cold. There was enough sun and enough rain. But
nothing grew. The farmer and his wife did not have
enough food for all their children. Everybody in
10   the village was hungry.

The boy became very
thin and he was often ill.

'Why won't the crops grow, husband? Our son is
always sick. We don't have enough food for him to get
15   better. What should we do?' asked the farmer's wife.

'Let's take him to the temple,' said the farmer. 'If he
stays here with us, he will die. Let's ask the monks to

take him. They will look after him. They will feed him well. And they will teach him to read and write.'

The farmer's wife was sad. 'We'll never see our little boy again,' she said. She began to cry.

'But he will be alive,' said her husband. 'That's the important thing.'

Sadly the parents took the little boy to the temple. The Abbot welcomed them kindly.

'Why have you come?' the Abbot asked.

'All our crops have died,' replied the farmer. 'We haven't enough food. This is our youngest son. He is a good boy. His health is not good. Please let him stay here with you.'

'We'll see,' said the Abbot. He asked the boy three questions. What were those questions? Nobody can remember. But the boy answered quickly and cleverly. The Abbot listened carefully to the boy's answers.

'Very well, you can stay,' he said.

Sadly the parents said goodbye to their son.

'Be a good boy. Listen to the Abbot and obey him,' they said.

Life at the temple

The boy stood at the gate, waving goodbye. He felt very small and quite sad. But he didn't cry. He wanted to be brave.

Suddenly the Abbot was beside him. 'You'll be all
5 right, child,' said the Abbot. 'Can you read yet?'

The boy shook his head.

'You'll soon learn,' said the Abbot kindly. 'Just work hard and obey your teachers. Don't give the monks trouble. Now it's dinner time.'

10 The boy ate a big dinner. He was very hungry.

After dinner the boy bowed to the Abbot. Then an old monk took him to a long sleeping hall.

'Here is your bed,' he said. 'Sleep well.'

The boy put his clothes away. Then he put three
15 things beside his bed. There was a brush, a stick of black ink and a stone pot. He used the pot for mixing the ink with water. The boy loved drawing. And he loved drawing dragons most of all.

In the morning the boy got up and worked with the
20 monks. They did jobs in the temple and the garden. He helped to keep the temple clean. He did many different things. He was busy all day. The Abbot was pleased with him. The boy was tired and very hungry. He ate an enormous dinner and went to bed early.

25 The next morning the monks woke up early. The boy got up too. They went down to the great hall. There, they got a big surprise.

Someone had drawn pictures of dragons on the walls! There were cheerful dragons, angry dragons,
30 running dragons, dancing dragons and flying dragons. Some of the dragons were blowing fire out of their noses. There were big dragons and small dragons. They were very good pictures. The dragons looked full of life.

8
The Boy Who Drew Dragons:
Part Two

'Who drew these dragons?'

The Abbot was angry. 'Who drew these dragons?' he asked.

Monks looked at each other and shook their heads. The Abbot looked at the boy. He said nothing.

'Clean the walls,' the Abbot ordered. A young monk brought water and a brush. Carefully he washed the pictures away.

The next morning the monks came down to the great hall. The walls were clean and white.

'Good,' said the Abbot. 'No more dragons. I will read to you.'

He took a book from the shelf and opened it. On the first page of the book someone had drawn a picture. It was a picture of a dragon!

The Abbot opened another book. He found a picture of a dragon. The monks opened all the other books on the shelf. They found pictures of dragons in every book.

'Who is drawing dragons everywhere?' said one monk.

'It's never happened before,' said another. 'It must be the new boy!'

'Go to work,' the Abbot ordered. He turned to the boy. 'I need to talk to you.'

'Now, my child,' said the Abbot. 'Are the monks right? Did you draw those dragons?'

'Yes,' said the boy.

'But why?' asked the Abbot.

5 ## The boy leaves the temple

'I'm sorry,' said the boy. 'I see a nice white wall and I want to draw. I see an empty page in a book and I have to draw. I see dragons! I have to draw them. There they are — alive, and beautiful. Their eyes
10 shine, their legs move and their tails wave. Please understand.'

'You draw well,' said the Abbot. 'The dragons are full of life. Perhaps one day you will be an artist. But this is a temple, not a school. You must do your work,
15 my child. You must obey the monks. If you can't do that, you must leave. Your parents brought you here because they love you. There is no food at home. They want you to live. Please be a good boy. Don't draw any more dragons.'

20 For two days all went well. The boy worked hard. The monks were pleased with him.

But on the third night he woke up again ... and drew!

He just wanted to draw dragons. That was all he could think about. He took his brush and his pot of ink.
25 He mixed some ink. He drew a beautiful dragon on the wall beside his bed.

In the morning all the monks saw the picture. The Abbot spoke to the boy.

'The gods have sent us a sign,' he said. 'You must
30 leave here. The gods will show you the way. Remember one thing. Stay in small places. Big places are not safe for you.'

The boy did not understand. He bowed to the Abbot and thanked him. He put his things in his bag. Then he left the temple.

The empty temple

It was late autumn and the sky was grey. A cold wind was blowing. The wind blew through the trees. The boy felt cold and a little afraid.

'Where can I go? Where can I sleep? What can I eat?'

He walked and walked. At last he saw another temple.

'It looks very big,' the boy thought. 'Perhaps the monks will let me stay. Perhaps they need an artist!'

The boy came nearer to the temple. There were no lights in the windows.

'That's strange,' he thought.

The temple was empty because a demon lived there. The boy did not know that — how could he know?

Sometimes travellers went into that empty temple. And the demon would come out of his hiding place. He would surprise the travellers. Then he would bite them with his long yellow teeth!

15

20

25

30

9

The Boy Who Drew Dragons:
Part Three

The screen

It was getting dark. The boy was tired, cold and hungry. He walked up to the great doors and knocked. Bang! Bang! Each knock was like thunder. But nobody answered.

'Where is everybody?' he said to himself. 'Perhaps the monks are out working in the fields. But it's getting dark. They must come back soon. Well, I'll go in and wait for them.'

He pushed the enormous doors. Creak! 'The hinges of these doors are rusty,' thought the boy.

The boy stepped inside the great, dark building. Spiders' webs brushed his face.

'This place is very dirty,' thought the boy. 'Perhaps the monks are too busy. I know! While I am waiting I'll clean the place up. Then the monks will be pleased. They'll let me stay.'

He found a lamp in a corner. He lit it and looked for a brush. He found one; and soon the spiders' webs were gone.

Now he was tired, cold and hungry. He was also a little afraid. 'Where are the monks? They must come back soon,' thought the boy.

Just then, he saw something white at one end of the great hall. It was a screen. It was made of wood, with hinges that folded. On the wood were sheets of beautiful white rice paper.

Noises in the night

The boy was excited. He put his lamp on the floor. He took his ink stick and his little pot and went outside. Creak! went the rusty hinges. Near the temple he found a stream. He put water in the pot and went into the temple again. Quickly he mixed his ink. Then he picked up his brush and drew — DRAGONS!

He stood back and looked at his work. There were dragons all over the beautiful white screen. In the light of the lamp the dragons looked almost alive.

'These are my best dragons,' the boy thought. And for a short time he forgot to feel tired, or cold, or hungry.

Then he remembered the Abbot's words: 'Stay in small places. Big places are not safe for you.' The temple was very large. The boy felt afraid. He found a cupboard with a thin paper door. He went inside and shut the door. Soon he was asleep.

In the middle of the night the boy woke. There were screams and growls. There were bangs and crashes. Something was happening — but what? The boy lay in his cupboard listening. What was happening? He did not really want to know ... Then everything was quiet. *5*

The demon is dead

In the morning the light of the sun shone through the thin paper door of the cupboard. The boy opened it. He listened. Everything was quiet.

Bravely the boy stepped out of the cupboard. He *10* looked around. There was blood on the walls and on the floor. And there, in a pool of blood, lay a demon. It was twenty feet long, with enormous teeth. It was dead.

'Who — or what — saved me from this demon? Why *15* didn't it kill me?' thought the boy.

Then he saw the screen. His dragons were still there. But there was blood on the screen. Every dragon had blood on its teeth and on its long, sharp claws.

The boy went back to the Abbot and told him his *20* story.

'I understand now, my child,' said the Abbot. 'The demon stopped the crops from growing. You and your dragons killed the demon. Now the demon is dead. The crops will grow again. You have saved your family and *25* all your neighbours. You are a hero, my child. You must go home to your parents. They will be very happy.'

The boy went home. His parents were very happy to see him. And the Abbot was right. Suddenly the fields were green and lovely. The crops grew tall. There was *30* plenty of food. Everybody was happy.

The boy became a famous artist. Everyone in Japan

knew about him. Every day he took his brush and drew
— what?

Can you guess? Yes, you can!

10

Dick Whittington and His Cat:
Part One

'The streets of London are full of gold'

Have you read *The Pied Piper of Hamelin* yet? Hamelin is a real town. But was there ever a real Pied Piper? Nobody knows. Now here is the story of Dick Whittington. Was there ever a real Dick Whittington? Well, there was a person called Richard Whittington, and 'Dick' is a short way of saying 'Richard'. He lived about six hundred years ago. He was Lord Mayor of London not once, but three times!

Perhaps Richard Whittington was the boy in this story. No one knows if he ever had a cat, and most people think he was never really poor. But this is still a good story!

Long ago, there was a boy called Dick Whittington. He lived in a small village a long way from London. His parents were dead and he was very poor.

His best friend was an enormous black cat called Tom. Dick was often hungry, but Tom always had enough to eat. Tom was a quick and clever cat. His claws and teeth were sharp. Every night Tom went hunting. He caught rats and mice. Sometimes he caught a rabbit and brought it to Dick.

One day a neighbour said to Dick, 'Go to London, my boy. The streets of London are full of gold.' He meant there was plenty of money there.

'Perhaps he's right, Tom,' said Dick.

5 The cat mewed. He looked at Dick with his big green eyes. 'But I can't leave you here. Let's go together.'

Dick and Tom did not have any money to get a carriage. They had to walk to London.

It was a long journey. At last they got as far as
10 Highgate, which was then just outside London. They sat down to rest. In front of them was the city. They could see all the houses and shops. They could see many churches and large buildings. They could see the river Thames, with many ships on it. They could hear
15 the noise of London too, and the sound of church bells ringing. Dick listened for a while. Then he said, 'Come on, Tom. We have got work to do. We have to find that gold!'

Dick and Tom walked all around London, looking
20 for gold. But they did not find any gold in the streets. At the end of the day, Dick and Tom were hungry and tired. That night Dick fell asleep on the steps of a big house. Tom sat beside him.

A rich merchant

25 The next morning a servant opened the door. She found a boy and a cat on the steps.

'Sorry,' said Dick. 'We're just going.'

Just then a man came to the door. His name was Fitzwarren. He was a rich merchant. He had a ship,
30 which travelled around the world selling things.

'Who's there, Mary?' he asked the servant.

'Only a beggar, sir. And a cat too. They were asleep on your steps. Go away!' she shouted to Dick. 'And take your nasty cat with you!'

Mr Fitzwarren had a kind heart. 'Wait,' he said to the servant. Then he spoke to Dick. 'What's your name, boy?' he asked.

'Dick Whittington, sir.'

Mr Fitzwarren took out his purse. He wanted to give Dick a penny. Then a girl came to the door. Her name was Alice. She was Mr Fitzwarren's daughter.

'Who's this, Father?'

'Only a poor boy.'

Then Alice saw Tom.

'What a beautiful cat!' she said. 'What's his name?'

'Tom.'

'Where did you find him?'

'In our village. He was very small then. A nasty boy wanted to throw him in the river. I knocked the boy down and I took the cat home with me.'

'Father,' said Alice, 'please may Dick and Tom stay here? You said yesterday, "Mary needs help in the kitchen." Father, please!'

'Very well, Alice.' He turned to Dick. 'Work hard and obey Mary and you'll be all right. Can your cat catch rats and mice?'

'Oh yes, sir.'

'That's good. We need a good rat-catcher.'

So Dick and Tom went to work in Mr Fitzwarren's kitchen.

11
Dick Whittington and His Cat:
Part Two

'Turn again, Whittington'

One day Mr Fitzwarren came to the servants' hall. A tall man with a black beard was with him.

'I am sending a ship to Barbary. This is Bob Brown.
5 He is the captain of the ship. We want to fill the ship with useful things to sell. Have you got anything? Perhaps you will make a lot of money.'

Every servant had something — except Dick. Then the captain saw Tom.

10 'Whose cat is that? And can he catch rats?'

'He's mine, sir,' said Dick. 'And he's a great rat-catcher.'

'Our ship needs a cat. Will you sell him to me?'

'Never, sir — but may he have a job on your ship?'

'Very well. He must catch all the rats, and he must bring me their tails. I'll pay a penny for every tail.'

So Tom became a ship's cat and sailed away to Barbary.

Two years passed. Time passed slowly for Dick. This was not a happy time for him. He missed Tom. He often worried about him, too. 'Did Tom like living on a ship? Was the captain kind to him?' he thought.

Then a new cook arrived. He was cruel to Dick. He did not give him enough to eat. And sometimes he beat him.

Dick was very unhappy. One day he said to himself, 'I shall go back to my old home. I was often hungry there, but nobody beat me.'

He started on his long journey.

He was almost out of the city. There were green fields in front of him. Just then he heard the sound of church bells. Dick listened to their music. Words came into his head.

'Turn again, Whittington,' the bells sang. 'Turn again, Whittington, Lord Mayor of London.'

'Lord Mayor of London?' said Dick. 'That's silly. But perhaps I should go back to London after all.'

With the music of the bells singing in his ears, the boy walked back towards London.

Dick is rich

Later that night, Dick arrived outside Mr Fitzwarren's house. Suddenly a black shape jumped out of an open window. It landed on the step in front of Dick.

'Tom!' shouted Dick. 'Is it really you?'

Dick held Tom in his arms. The big black cat rubbed his face against Dick's arm. They were both pleased and happy to see each other.

'Tom, I've missed you! I'm happy you are home.'

Tom rubbed his face against Dick's arm again, and mewed happily.

The door opened and Mr Fitzwarren came out. 'Dick, there you are! Where have you been? We looked for you everywhere.'

'Sorry, sir. I — I went for a walk.'

'Well, my ship has come back from Barbary. Captain Brown wants to talk to you.'

'Hello Dick,' said the captain. 'I made you a promise about rats. Do you remember?'

5   'Yes, sir — a penny for every tail.'

'Well, your cat killed a hundred rats on the ship. Here is the money. But that's not all. We arrived in Barbary — and the town was full of rats. There were rats everywhere, and no cats to kill them.'

10   'I showed your cat to the King of Barbary. The King said, "I'll give you a piece of gold for every tail." Well, your cat did a very good job. He worked very hard. There aren't any rats in Barbary now. The King kept his promise and now you're rich!'

15   He gave Dick a bag of gold.

'Tom, you're a hero!' cried Dick. 'We're rich now.' The cat looked up at Dick with his big green eyes. He mewed happily. Dick smiled. He was happy.

Dick became a merchant. He and Mr Fitzwarren 20 worked happily together. Later, Dick married Alice. And one day the other merchants chose him to be their Lord Mayor. The music of the church bells was right — Dick became the Lord Mayor of London. And Tom? He rode in the Lord Mayor's carriage beside Dick.

12
Where Do Stories Come From?

'Tell us a story'

Manza and Zenze lived in Africa. They lived in a small village with their children. Manza made baskets and hats. Zenze loved to draw pictures.

Every night their children said, 'Tell us a story.' And every night Manza and Zenze shook their heads sadly. They did not know any stories.

One day Zenze said to his wife, 'You must go and find some stories for our children.' So Manza said goodbye to the children and went to look for some stories.

She looked everywhere, and she asked many people and animals. None of them could help her. Then an elephant said, 'Perhaps the sea eagle can help you. He is the king of the birds.'

Manza found the sea eagle sitting on a rock. He held a fish in his claws.

'Excuse me,' called Manza. The sea eagle looked round — and dropped his fish.

'Foolish woman!' he said angrily. 'Now I've lost my dinner. What do you want?'

'Great Sea Eagle, I need your help. Where can I find stories? Please help me.'

'I can't help you, woman. But I will ask the sea turtle. He knows all the secrets of the deep, dark sea. Wait for me here.'

The magic people

At last the sea eagle came back. He landed on the rock beside Manza. Suddenly there was a loud splash. A green head came out of the water, then a dark shell. It was as big as a table.

'Woman,' said the turtle, 'climb on my back. I will take you to the Land of the Magic People under the sea.'

Manza thanked the sea eagle. Then she climbed onto the turtle's back. Together they swam down, down, down ...

Everything was strange and beautiful. The fish and shells were all the colours of the rainbow. There were lots of strange animals with many legs.

At last they found the King and Queen of the Magic People. Manza bowed to them. She told them she was looking for stories.

'We have many stories,' said the Queen kindly. 'We could give you some. But what will you give us?'

'Well,' said Manza, 'I can make baskets and hats ...'

'We don't need baskets. We don't need hats. We would like a picture of your home and your people. We can never visit your world. We'd like to know something about it.'

'Oh yes,' said Manza. 'I can do that. Thank you!'

She bowed again. Then she climbed onto the turtle's back. They swam back to the rock.

'Please come again in seven days,' she said to the turtle.

Manza told her family all about her adventures. She told them about the Land of the Magic People. She told them about the King and Queen. Then she told them about the picture.

Zenze started work. First he took a large, thin, flat stone. He drew pictures on the stone. Then, he picked

up his sharpest knife. He cut deep lines in the stone. He
worked hard.

Manza's first story

On the seventh day the picture was
5 ready. Zenze showed it to his family.
They saw the village, the fields, the
gardens and all the people.

'What a clever artist you are,
Zenze,' said Manza.

10 They carried the picture to the
rock. The sea turtle was waiting for Manza.

Carefully Zenze tied the picture to the turtle's back.
Manza climbed on. They swam down to the Land of the
Magic People.

15 The King and Queen were very happy. They asked
Manza to talk about the picture. Soon they knew all
about the village.

'Here is a present for you,' said the Queen. She gave
Manza a beautiful string of shells. She put them round
20 Manza's neck.

'We promised you some stories,' said the King. He
gave her a big, beautiful shell. 'All the stories are inside
this shell,' he said. 'Just hold the shell near your ear
and listen. You will hear your story.'

25 'Thank you, thank you!' said Manza. Then she
climbed on the turtle's back again. They swam back up
to the rock.

They came to dry land. All the people in the village
were there.

30 'Manza,' they said, 'please tell us a story.'

So Manza held the shell near her ear and began.

'Once upon a time, long ago ...'

Questions and Activities

1 The Pied Piper of Hamelin: Part One

Match the description to the right person or animal.
The first one has been done for you.

1 He had long yellow hair and big blue eyes.
   The Pied Piper

2 He was a fat little man, who liked wearing
   beautiful robes.

3 They had sharp claws and long yellow teeth.

4 They talked and talked with the Mayor for hours.

5 They ran away when they saw the rats.

2 The Pied Piper of Hamelin: Part Two

Which of these sentences are true, and which are
false?

		T	F
1	The Pied Piper led the rats to the river by playing his pipe.	☐	☐
2	The Mayor gave the Pied Piper a thousand dollars.	☐	☐
3	The Pied Piper had to get rid of spiders in Baghdad.	☐	☐
4	The Pied Piper took the bag of money.	☐	☐
5	The side of the mountain opened like a door.	☐	☐

3 Rip Van Winkle: Part One

Complete the sentences with the words from the box.

farm	lazy	stories	Wolf
Judith	Rip	toys	

1 Rip Van Winkle had a son called ▢▢▢▢▢ and a daughter called ▢▢▢▢▢ .

2 He made ▢▢▢▢▢ for the children and told them exciting ▢▢▢▢▢ .

3 His wife thought he was ▢▢▢▢▢ .

4 He did not like working on his own ▢▢▢▢▢ .

5 His best friend was ▢▢▢▢▢ , his dog.

4 Rip Van Winkle: Part Two

Which of these sentences are true, and which are false?

	T	F
1 Rip and his wife were hunting in the mountains.	▢	▢
2 He saw a stranger in a deep, dark valley full of rocks.	▢	▢
3 The stranger was tall and had a white beard.	▢	▢
4 They came to a small valley, where Rip saw some men in old-fashioned clothes playing tennis.	▢	▢
5 Rip drank too much liquor and fell asleep.	▢	▢

5 Rip Van Winkle: Part Three

Put these sentences in the right order.

1 Many people in the village were surprised when they saw him. ☐

2 He arrived at his own house. ☐

3 Rip went home because he wanted his breakfast. ☐

4 Rip went to The King's Head. ☐

5 A small crowd were talking about the new government. ☐

6 Rip Van Winkle: Part Four

Answer these questions with the names from the box.

Derrick Van Bummel   Nicholas Vedder
Hendrick Hudson   Peter Vanderdonk
Judith Gardener

1 What is the name of the old innkeeper?

2 What is the name of the old schoolteacher?

3 What is the name of Rip's daughter?

4 Who comes back for one day, in every twenty years?

5 Whose father saw the men in old-fashioned Dutch clothes once?

7 The Boy Who Drew Dragons: Part One

Which of these sentences are true, and which are false?

		T	F
1	Everyone in the village was hungry.	☐	☐
2	The boy loved drawing horses and elephants.	☐	☐
3	The farmer's youngest child became very thin and he was often ill.	☐	☐
4	The boy slept in a little room in the temple.	☐	☐
5	The boy drew dragons with a pencil.	☐	☐

8 The Boy Who Drew Dragons: Part Two

Put these sentences in the right order.

1 At last, he entered an empty temple. ☐

2 The Abbot opened a book and found a picture of a dragon. ☐

3 The boy drew a dragon beside his bed. ☐

4 The boy walked and walked. ☐

5 The Abbot told the boy to leave the temple. ☐

9 The Boy Who Drew Dragons: Part Three

Fill in the gaps with the words from the box.

demon	hinges	stream
dragons	screen	thunder

1 The boy knocked on the door. Each knock was like
          .

2 The ▓▓▓▓▓▓ on the door were rusty.

3 The boy went to a ▓▓▓▓▓▓ near the temple and brought back some water.

4 There was a white ▓▓▓▓▓▓ in the room made of wood and rice paper.

5 The boy drew ▓▓▓▓▓▓ on the screen.

6 The dragons saved the boy from the ▓▓▓▓▓▓.

10 Dick Whittington and His Cat: Part One

Complete the sentences with the words from the box.

carriage	poor	steps
cat	rabbit	

1 Dick's parents were dead and he was very ▓▓▓▓▓▓.

2 Tom was an enormous black ▓▓▓▓▓▓.

3 Sometimes Tom caught a ▓▓▓▓▓▓ and brought it to Dick.

4 Dick and Tom had to walk to London. They did not have any money to get a ▓▓▓▓▓▓.

5 Dick fell asleep on the ▓▓▓▓▓▓ of a big house.

11 Dick Whittington and His Cat: Part Two

Which of these sentences are true, and which are false?

<table>
<tr><td></td><td></td><td>T</td><td>F</td></tr>
<tr><td>1</td><td>The new cook was kind to Dick.</td><td>☐</td><td>☐</td></tr>
<tr><td>2</td><td>Dick was unhappy and he set off for home.</td><td>☐</td><td>☐</td></tr>
<tr><td>3</td><td>The King of Barbary gave a penny for every rat's tail.</td><td>☐</td><td>☐</td></tr>
<tr><td>4</td><td>Mr Fitzwarren gave the money to Dick.</td><td>☐</td><td>☐</td></tr>
<tr><td>5</td><td>Dick became a merchant and was later chosen to be Lord Mayor.</td><td>☐</td><td>☐</td></tr>
</table>

12 Where Do Stories Come From?

Who said these things?

1 'Tell us a story.' •   • **a** The elephant

2 'I will ask the sea turtle.' •   • **b** The children

3 'Perhaps the sea eagle can help you.' •   • **c** The sea eagle

4 'Climb on my back.' •   • **d** The sea turtle

5 'But what will you give us?' •   • **e** Manza

6 'All the stories are inside this shell.' •   • **f** The Queen

7 'Find some stories for our children.' •   • **g** Zenze

8 'I can make baskets and hats.' •   • **h** The King

Book Report

Now write a book report to display in the library or your classroom. These questions will help you.

Title

Type What type of story is your book?

- Adventure
- Classic
- Crime
- Detective story
- Fairy tale
- Horror and suspense
- Mystery
- Play
- Romance
- Science fiction and fantasy
- Short story
- Others

Characters   Who are the main characters in the book?

Main characters   Describe the main characters.
What do they look like?
What are they like?

Story   What is the story about?
Remember not to give the ending away!

My comments   What did you think of the story?
Did you enjoy it?
Would you recommend this book to your classmates?

Visit the website and download the book report template
www.oupchina.com.hk/elt/oper

OXFORD PROGRESSIVE ENGLISH READERS

The Hound of the Baskervilles
Sir Arthur Conan Doyle

The Merchant of Venice and Other
Stories from Shakespeare's Plays
Edited by David Foulds

The Missing Scientist
S. F. Stevens

The Pickwick Papers
Charles Dickens

The Red Badge of Courage
Stephen Crane

Robinson Crusoe
Daniel Defoe

Silas Marner
George Eliot

Stories from Shakespeare's
Histories
Retold by Katherine Mattock

A Tale of Two Cities
Charles Dickens

Tales of Crime and Detection
Edited by David Foulds

Two Boxes of Gold and Other
Stories
Charles Dickens

LEVEL 4

Dr Jekyll and Mr Hyde and Other
Stories
Robert Louis Stevenson

Far from the Madding Crowd
Thomas Hardy

From Russia, With Love
Ian Fleming

The Gifts and Other Stories
O. Henry and Others

The Good Earth
Pearl S. Buck

The Great Gatsby
F. Scott Fitzgerald

Journey to the Centre of the Earth
Jules Verne

King Solomon's Mines
H. Rider Haggard

Mansfield Park
Jane Austen

The Moonstone
Wilkie Collins

A Night of Terror and Other
Strange Tales
Guy de Maupassant

Othello and Other Stories from
Shakespeare's Plays
Edited by David Foulds

The Picture of Dorian Gray
Oscar Wilde

Seven Stories
H. G. Wells

Tales of Mystery and Imagination
Edgar Allan Poe

Tess of the d'Urbervilles
Thomas Hardy

The Thirty-nine Steps
John Buchan

Twenty Thousand Leagues Under
the Sea
Jules Verne

The War of the Worlds
H. G. Wells

The Woman in White
Wilkie Collins

You Only Live Twice
Ian Fleming

LEVEL 5

The Diamond as Big as the Ritz
and Other Stories
F. Scott Fitzgerald

Dracula
Bram Stoker

Dragon Seed
Pearl S. Buck

Frankenstein
Mary Shelley

Kidnapped
Robert Louis Stevenson

Lorna Doone
R. D. Blackmore

The Mayor of Casterbridge
Thomas Hardy

The Old Wives' Tale
Arnold Bennett

Pride and Prejudice
Jane Austen

The Stalled Ox and Other Stories
Saki

Three Men in a Boat
Jerome K. Jerome

Vanity Fair
William Thackeray

Wuthering Heights
Emily Brontë